T0054346

ANXIETY RELIEF

WORKBOOK for KIDS

40 Mindfulness, CBT, and ACT Activities to Find Peace from Anxiety and Worry

DR. AGNES SELINGER, PhD

Illustrations by Claudio Cerri

ROCKRIDGE
PRESS

Copyright © 2021 by Rockridge Press, Emeryville, California

No part of this publication may be reproduced, stored in a retrieval system, or transmitted in any form or by any means, electronic, mechanical, photocopying, recording, scanning, or otherwise, except as permitted under Sections 107 or 108 of the 1976 United States Copyright Act, without the prior written permission of the Publisher. Requests to the Publisher for permission should be addressed to the Permissions Department, Rockridge Press, 6005 Shellmound Street, Suite 175, Emeryville, CA 94608.

Limit of Liability/Disclaimer of Warranty: The Publisher and the author make no representations or warranties with respect to the accuracy or completeness of the contents of this work and specifically disclaim all warranties, including without limitation warranties of fitness for a particular purpose. No warranty may be created or extended by sales or promotional materials. The advice and strategies contained herein may not be suitable for every situation. This work is sold with the understanding that the Publisher is not engaged in rendering medical, legal, or other professional advice or services. If professional assistance is required, the services of a competent professional person should be sought. Neither the Publisher nor the author shall be liable for damages arising herefrom. The fact that an individual, organization, or website is referred to in this work as a citation and/or potential source of further information does not mean that the author or the Publisher endorses the information the individual, organization, or website may provide or recommendations they/it may make. Further, readers should be aware that websites listed in this work may have changed or disappeared between when this work was written and when it is read.

For general information on our other products and services or to obtain technical support, please contact our Customer Care Department within the United States at (866) 744-2665, or outside the United States at (510) 253-0500.

Rockridge Press publishes its books in a variety of electronic and print formats. Some content that appears in print may not be available in electronic books, and vice versa.

TRADEMARKS: Rockridge Press and the Rockridge Press logo are trademarks or registered trademarks of Callisto Media Inc. and/or its affiliates, in the United States and other countries, and may not be used without written permission. All other trademarks are the property of their respective owners. Rockridge Press is not associated with any product or vendor mentioned in this book.

Interior and Cover Designer: Tricia Jang
Art Producer: Janice Ackerman
Editor: Andrea Leptinsky
Production Editor: Andrew Yackira
Production Manager: Holly Haydash

Illustration: © 2021 Claudio Cerri
Author Photo: Courtesy of Valérie Louise Levin

ISBN: Print 978-1-64876-932-0
Printed in Canada
R0

This book is
dedicated to my loving family—
thank you for your unconditional
love and support.

CONTENTS

• •

A LETTER TO
KIDS

• •

Dear Kids,

Do you ever feel like you have butterflies in your tummy before school? Do you ever feel like something bad will happen? Like when your parent turns off the lights at bedtime? Do you ask adults a lot of questions about the future? Believe it or not, there is a name for this feeling, called "anxiety." The good news is that anxiety is a feeling that everybody has. Your mom, dad, brother, sister, teacher, and neighbor all feel anxious at some point, too! This book will teach you about anxiety and how to handle it so that it doesn't upset you.

You might feel anxious during different parts of the day. Some kids feel anxious as soon as they wake up. Their minds think ahead to what might happen at school. Other kids feel anxious when they are in class. They might worry about who will pick them up after school or if they will get to have a playdate. Some kids feel anxious before starting their homework or right before bed. They might worry about making a mistake on their homework or worry about what will happen at school the next day. The goal of this book is to teach you how to deal with your anxiety, no matter when you feel anxious, using exercises that will teach you new skills. Think of each exercise as a new superpower that you can use to handle anxiety. Once you've gone through all the exercises, pick the ones you like the best. That way you can make your own set of super-powers and be your own special superhero.

A LETTER TO
GROWN-UPS

· ·

Dear Parents and Guardians,

This book is a resource to help your child learn about anxiety, normalize their experience, and teach them how to manage it effectively using change and acceptance-based skills. The strategies outlined in this book are based on cognitive behavioral therapy (CBT), acceptance and commitment therapy (ACT), and mindfulness, which are evidence-based treatments. This book is also a resource for you to learn about these therapeutic approaches and how to recognize the signs of anxiety not only in your child but in you, too. To learn more, see Just for Parents (page 100).

Anxiety is actually a helpful and healthy emotion, and that is the first thing your child will learn. However, sometimes anxiety can grow to the point of overwhelming your child. For example, your child may be anxious about going to school. If your child's anxiety is not too high, you may be able to successfully reassure them and they move on. But when anxiety is high, your child will ask many questions in an effort to find reassurance and continue to feel anxious despite your best attempts. This book is for those moments when anxiety is high. The hope is that by learning to manage anxiety on their own, your child will boost their self-esteem and confidence.

Children who experience anxiety frequently have a high need for predictability and comfort. If your child feels uncomfortable, their brain signals a need for change, to fix this immediately so that they are comfortable again. That's an excellent system when it comes to physical needs but not necessarily helpful with regard to anxiety. Often the things kids do to feel less anxious in the moment can actually make anxiety worse in the long run. Anxiety is an emotion that is meant to signal information. It's helpful for your child to receive this information even though it may not feel good. With practice, your child will learn how to tolerate anxiety using the skills outlined in this book while still engaging in things they need to do.

This book is intended for children who experience anxiety in many situations. Some common situations may include difficulties separating from parents, social anxiety, specific fears like fear of the dark or of natural phenomena like thunderstorms, and fears about their academic performance, among others. The good news is that the skills your child will learn in this book can be used anytime and anywhere.

Your attention and actions influence your child more than anyone else. As a parent or guardian, it is helpful for you to share that you, too, get anxious sometimes. Share examples that won't cause additional anxiety, such as "I sometimes worry about what my coworkers think of me" rather than "I worry we don't have enough money to pay the bills." This will help your child realize that they are not alone in experiencing worries. As you go through the workbook together with your child, you will read about different skills to manage anxiety. You can help your child even further by sharing if you tried some of the skills presented in this book when you felt anxious. This will help keep your child motivated to practice the exercises.

This book is organized around your child's routine to help them manage anxiety at various times throughout their day. The four approaches used in this book offer concrete skills that your child can learn to help deal with their anxiety. These skills are presented as "superpowers" in this book and are: (1) Changing Worries, (2) Being Brave, (3) Getting Unstuck, and (4) Laser Focus. The skills are aimed at children aged 6 to 9 and taught through 40 exercises, or 8 exercises per chapter. Please note that although certain exercises are suggested to be used at a specific time of day, the skills can be used anytime. What is most important is to identify which skills are most useful to your child, to practice them, and to incorporate them into your everyday routine.

Learning these skills is just like learning any new task; it takes some time, and you have to practice in order to feel comfortable doing that task. When learning to read, your child first learns the letters of the alphabet, puts letters together to form words, and eventually learns how to read words together in a sentence. Learning to read is a process just like learning to manage anxiety. The goal of this book is to provide the tools and support your child needs to develop inner calm and a sense of pride. And that can apply to you, too!

CHAPTER 1

What Is Worry?

WHY DO I FEEL WORRIED?

A "worry" is a thought you might have about something that could happen in the future. Maybe you've had a hard time sleeping because you were thinking *a lot* about how something bad could happen in the dark. Or maybe you have to speak in front of your class, and you worry that you will forget what to say. These are all different types of worries. Some worries get stuck in our brain, and we can't stop thinking about them. When we pay close attention to a worry, it actually grows and becomes bigger. It's just like when you zoom in on your computer screen and the pictures and words become larger.

Did you know that anxiety is a feeling that's meant to protect you from danger? A dangerous situation could be a person standing near a hungry lion. Anxiety protects us from danger in three different ways, which are fight, flight, or freeze. "Fight" is when anxiety gives us a burst of energy to yell and wave our arms to scare the lion away. "Flight" is when anxiety makes us run away from the hungry lion. "Freeze" is when anxiety makes us hide behind the bushes and watch the lion walk past. You may experience one, two, or all three of them when you feel nervous. These three actions caused by anxiety can help protect you from danger!

Think of a video game where you have to find bad guys. Anxiety is like a special scanner that helps you find them. It's pretty useful to have! But sometimes that scanner doesn't work well. It may tell you that some of the good guys are actually bad guys. The next thing you know, it looks like everyone is a bad guy! This is what happens when we have too much anxiety. The feeling tricks us into believing some things are true when they are not. Some of our scanners are more sensitive and go off more easily than others. Thankfully, you will learn superpowers to get your scanner working again!

FIND THE GOOD IN ANXIETY

Now, it's your turn! Match the words on the left with the best fill-in-the-blank sentence on the right. This will help you learn the different ways your anxiety can be helpful.

1. Ducking

A. _____ out of the way of a moving car

2. Boat

B. _____ from a ball headed straight for your head

3. Jumping

C. Jumping off a sinking _____

4. Running

D. Not _____ a growling dog

5. Petting

E. _____ out of a building that is on fire

Answers: A: Jumping, B: Ducking, C: Boat, D: Petting, E: Running

MY WORRIES

Draw or list three different worries you might have. Remember: worries are the words you say to yourself about the future. If you're not sure, ask a trusted adult.

1.

2.

3.

WHAT CAN I DO ABOUT MY ANXIETY?

There are lots of superpowers that can help you deal with your worries and feelings of anxiety. In this book, we will focus on four different super-powers we can use to make us feel less anxious.

CHANGING WORRIES

This superpower will change the shape of your worries. Sometimes a worry feels scary, but when you stop and think about it, it's not scary at all. For example, you may have been worried about monsters under your bed when you go to sleep but then you thought about it and realized that every time your parent or guardian checked under the bed there has never been a monster. Not once! Poof! Your worry has now changed.

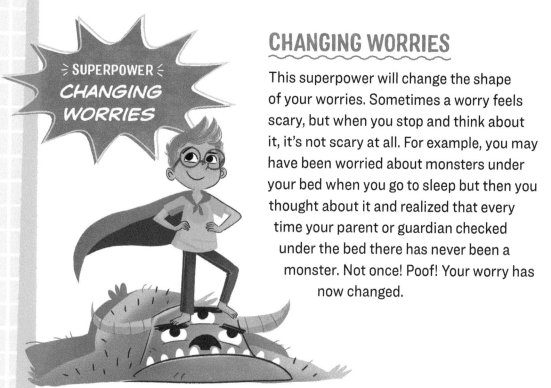

SUPERPOWER
CHANGING WORRIES

BEING BRAVE

The superpower of bravery means facing your anxiety. It might feel scary, but you'll gather up all of your courage and say to your anxiety, "No, you won't scare me!" For example, maybe you felt anxious about going to a friend's birthday party. Instead of staying home, you gathered up all of your bravery and said, "I am going to the party!" Guess what? You went and you had a great time! Nice job! You just faced your anxiety and had lots of fun.

GETTING UNSTUCK

This superpower teaches you how to interact with your thoughts differently so that you can focus on doing the things you love. Sometimes when we think about something that makes us anxious, we can't do anything else. The anxious thought makes us feel stuck. With this superpower, you'll learn to get unstuck! For example, maybe you're at the beach and love playing in the sand and water. But a fly is buzzing around your head. You can spend all day annoyed by the flies or you can focus your attention on the sand, water, and having fun instead!

⚡ SUPERPOWER ⚡
LASER FOCUS

LASER FOCUS

The laser focus superpower is all about being able to focus and control your attention on the present. For example, when you take deep belly breaths, you are concentrating only on your breathing. When you focus on breathing, you are focusing on being present. That means there is no room for worries. How cool is that?!

By practicing these superpowers, you will get better at handling your worries and feelings of anxiety.

DRAW A SUPERHERO

What does a superhero battling their own anxiety look like to you? In the boxes below, draw a superhero for each of our new superpowers.

CHANGING WORRIES	BEING BRAVE
GETTING UNSTUCK	LASER FOCUS

GETTING TO KNOW MYSELF AND MY WORRIES

Let's learn how to tell if you are feeling anxious. The good news is that your body sends signals to let you know that you are feeling anxious. With practice you will get better at knowing when your body is sending you a signal. Some examples of signals your body may send you are: feeling like you have butterflies in your tummy; a headache; feeling tightness in your arms, shoulders, and legs; feeling sweaty; feeling like your heart is beating really fast or like you're breathing really fast.

Another way your brain sends a signal that you are feeling anxious is when you have lots of worries about things before they happen, like "Who will be at my friend's birthday party?" or "How long will it take to get to my friend's house?" You may be asking a lot of questions looking for reassurance, like "Did I do that right?", "Are you sure you will pick me up from school today?", or "Will I be okay?"

Now that you've learned how to tell if you are anxious, the next step is learning how to tell WHAT is making you feel anxious. One great way to figure this out is to ask yourself, "What just happened?" when you start feeling anxious. If you're not sure, that's okay. These next exercises will help you find out what just happened.

THINGS THAT MAKE ME FEEL ANXIOUS

Here is a list of things that make some of us anxious. First, go through this list and circle the ones that make you anxious. Then take a look at the items you circled and rate how scary each item is from 1 to 10, with 1 being the least scary and 10 being the scariest.

THINGS THAT MAKE ME FEEL ANXIOUS

RATING

Being away from my parents   - - - - - - - -

Thunder and lightning   - - - - - - - -

Being late   - - - - - - - -

Getting a shot at the doctor's office   - - - - - - - -

The dark   - - - - - - - -

Heights   - - - - - - - -

Bridges   - - - - - - - -

Bugs   - - - - - - - -

Going to the bathroom   - - - - - - - -

Not being able to fall asleep   - - - - - - - -

Tests or homework   - - - - - - - -

Fear that my teacher will be mad at me   - - - - - - - -

Fear that my parents will be mad at me   - - - - - - - -

Fear that my friends will be mean to me   - - - - - - - -

Fear of what my friends think of me   - - - - - - - -

Fear of breaking a rule   - - - - - - - -

Fear of making a mistake   - - - - - - - -

Escalators or elevators   - - - - - - - -

Water (pool, lake, or ocean)   - - - - - - - -

Loud noises   - - - - - - - -

My brother or sister will move or break my stuff   - - - - - - - -

Germs   - - - - - - - -

Getting sick   - - - - - - - -

Other _   - - - - - - - -

DRAWING MY ANXIETY

Let's draw! Draw a picture of your body. Then circle the areas of your body where you feel anxious.

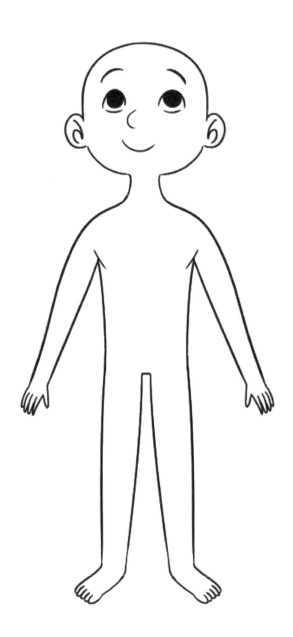

WHEN WORRIES PILE UP

Worries come in different sizes. Some worries are small and others are big. Small worries may sound like "I need to pack my backpack for school" and don't really bother us. But other worries feel really big and upset us, like "What if I forget my backpack at home?" Often you can tell if you are having a big worry when you notice your body trying to tell you about anxiety. Your body can do this through things like tummy aches or making your heart beat really fast.

Sometimes a worry can get stuck in your mind. Once it's stuck, you focus and zoom in on your worry. You may think, "What if I forget my backpack when I get to school?" All of a sudden, a lot of other worries start popping up as well: "My teacher will be so mad at me." "I won't be able to turn in my homework." "I won't get a check mark for my home-work." "My parents will be upset for having to bring my backpack to school." This is a worry pileup!

All these worries can make you feel very anxious. Anxiety can make it hard for you to fall asleep at night or eat breakfast in the morning because you are too worried about forgetting your backpack. When you have trouble doing things you usually do, this means that your anxiety is too high, and it's time to use your superpowers to lower that feeling. Are you ready to learn more about superpowers that can help you lower your anxiety?

WORRY VS. ANXIETY

In order to use superpowers to manage your anxiety, you first have to know when anxiety shows up. Let's practice getting better at noticing anxiety. For this exercise, write the letter "W" if you think the sentence is a worry or write the letter "A" if you think the sentence is the feeling of anxiety.

1.   Can I eat my cookie if it touched the ground? _ _ _ _ _ _ _ _

2.   I feel butterflies in my stomach. _ _ _ _ _ _ _ _

3.   I feel my heart beating fast. _ _ _ _ _ _ _ _

4.   Thunder means something bad will happen. _ _ _ _ _ _ _ _

5.   What if I'm late? _ _ _ _ _ _ _ _

Answers: 1, 4, and 5 are worries. 2 and 3 are anxiety.

SPOT THE WORRY!

Now it's time to practice telling the difference between a thought and a worry. Write the letter "W" by the sentence that sounds like a worry and the letter "T" by the sentence that is just a thought.

1.   **What if my parent forgets to pick me up after school?** _ _ _ _ _ _ _ _

2.   **The sky is blue.** _ _ _ _ _ _ _ _

3.   **Whales are big.** _ _ _ _ _ _ _ _

4.   **What if the other kids are mean?** _ _ _ _ _ _ _

5.   **Something bad will happen if I turn off the light.** _ _ _ _ _ _ _ _

Answers: 1, 4, and 5 are worries. 2 and 3 are thoughts.

MY NEW SUPERPOWERS

You've done a great job learning about worries, anxiety, and your new superpowers to keep them under control. Can you remember what the four superpowers are? Let's take a look:

1. **Changing Worries**

2. **Being Brave**

3. **Getting Unstuck**

4. **Laser Focus**

These superpowers will help you do different things like lessening your worries and learning how not to let your anxiety upset you. They can help you quiet your loud thoughts so that you can get back to doing the things you like. They will also let you stay focused on schoolwork! You can use these superpowers anytime—in the morning, at school, or right before bedtime.

Just like anything new you learn, you will have to practice. Remember when you learned how to read? First, you had to learn the letters of the alphabet. Then you put those letters together to read a word. With practice you put those words together to read a sentence. Next thing you knew, you were reading full sentences!

Learning a superpower is a skill just like reading. First, you have to complete the exercises as you read along in this book. Then you have to practice doing the exercises when you feel anxious during the day. Next thing you know, you will have memorized the exercise and will be able to do it in your head! Your parent or trusted adult can help you practice so that you can strengthen your superpowers.

KEEPING YOUR SUPERPOWERS SAFE

Your superpowers are special powers that make you uniquely you! Once you find out which superpowers are your favorites, draw them in this special supervault.

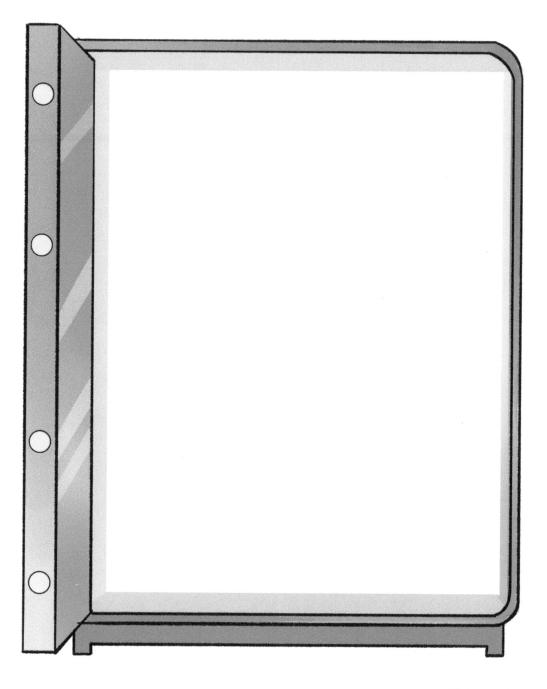

CHAPTER 2

Me in the Morning

HOW DO I FEEL IN THE MORNING?

So far, you have learned that everyone gets anxious. But WHEN you feel anxious is different for everybody. In the next few chapters, you will learn about what time of day you may feel more anxious. Once you know when your anxiety rises, then you and your superpowers can be prepared. Think of when you are playing a sport. If you know the other team is going to try to score a point, you can prepare yourself to block them from scoring. If you know that you get anxious in the morning, you can have your superpowers handy so that you can start your morning feeling less anxious.

Think back to the signals your body sends you when you are anxious. They can make it hard to get out of bed, get dressed, put your clothes on, eat breakfast, and go to school. If your mind is busy, it's easy to get distracted by your thoughts. If you start feeling anxious, you might feel like avoiding the things you usually do in the morning because it makes you feel uncomfortable. If this is happening, your anxiety scanner is probably sending you mixed signals.

Thankfully, the superpowers in this book can help you reset your anxiety scanner so you can get back to doing what you like. First, you will learn about what sets off your anxiety in the mornings. Then you will practice superpowers to handle anxiety.

THINGS I WORRY ABOUT IN THE MORNING

SUPERPOWER: *BEING BRAVE*

Let's learn what worries you in the morning. By using your Being Brave superpower, you can be open and honest about the things you're afraid of.

1. **In the list of Things I Worry About in the Morning, circle what makes you anxious in the morning.**

2. **Next, take a look at the items you circled and rate how anxious each one makes you from 1 to 10, with 1 being the least anxious and 10 being the most anxious.**

3. **Finally, put the worries you rated in order from the most anxiety provoking to the least anxiety provoking.**

Let's do an example together:

THINGS I WORRY ABOUT IN THE MORNING	RATING
Being late to school in the morning	8
Wondering what will happen today	5
My friends won't be at school today	6

Rank your worries from most anxiety provoking to least anxiety provoking:

Being late to school in the morning   _ _ _1_ _ _

Wondering what will happen today   _ _3_ _ _ _

My friends won't be at school today   _ _2_ _ _ _

Now it's your turn!

THINGS THAT MAKE ME WORRY IN THE MORNING   RATING

Being late to school in the morning   _ _ _ _ _ _ _

Wondering what will happen today   _ _ _ _ _ _ _

My friends won't be at school today   _ _ _ _ _ _ _

Wondering who will take me to school today   _ _ _ _ _ _ _

Wondering where my parents will be while I'm at school   _ _ _ _ _ _ _

Being unsure about what I will learn today   _ _ _ _ _ _ _

Not understanding what my teacher says today   _ _ _ _ _ _ _

Forgetting my backpack   _ _ _ _ _ _ _

Making a mistake on class assignments   _ _ _ _ _ _ _

Giving a wrong answer in class   _ _ _ _ _ _ _

Having to work in a group   _ _ _ _ _ _ _

Teacher asking me a question in class   _ _ _ _ _ _ _

continued »»

Things I Worry About in the Morning, *continued*

Another student will be mean to me   - - - - - - - -

Teacher will be mad at me   - - - - - - - -

Getting a tummy ache or headache   - - - - - - - -

Getting sick at school   - - - - - - - -

Eating lunch in front of others   - - - - - - - -

Using the bathroom at school   - - - - - - - -

Trusted adult will not pick me up after school   - - - - - - - -

Feeling like something bad will happen today   - - - - - - - -

I won't make the (soccer, gymnastics, baseball,
dance, basketball, hockey, etc.) team.   - - - - - - - -

Getting lost   - - - - - - - -

Transition from weekend to weekday   - - - - - - - -

Other _   - - - - - - - -

Rank your worries from most anxiety provoking to least anxiety provoking:

1. _

2. _

3. _

4. _

5. _

TENSION BUSTER

SUPERPOWER: *LASER FOCUS*

Let's practice the superpower of Laser Focus.

1. **While lying in bed, tense all of your muscles so they feel tight, like you're doing heavy work. Make a fist with both hands, make a muscle with both arms, bring your shoulders to your ears, tighten your belly, scrunch up your face, squeeze your calves, and point your toes all at once for as long as you can.**

2. **Release all of your muscles and RELAX. Take a deep belly breath here. Inhale through your nose and let your breath go all the way down to your belly button. Now exhale through your mouth and let all the air out of your lungs. Let go of all those muscles and lay limp like a noodle.**

Take notice of how you feel after tensing all your muscles. Do you feel tingling in your muscles? Do your muscles feel less tense? Do you feel a bit lighter? After your first try of tensing and relaxing your muscles, take note of how you feel.

3. **Repeat steps 1 and 2, tensing and relaxing, at least three times. When you're all done, notice how you feel. Are your muscles more relaxed?**

By focusing on tensing and relaxing your muscles, you are training your Laser Focus. This is a really helpful superpower to use if you have a tummy ache or headache or feel tension in your body when you wake up. Using Laser Focus in this exercise helps you release tension from your body.

BELLY BREATHING

SUPERPOWER: *LASER FOCUS*

This superpower will help you focus on the present so that you can be brave in the mornings.

1. **First, take a deep breath in through your nose. Feel the air tickle your nostrils, and feel your lungs fill with air. Imagine the air traveling all the way down to your belly button and watch your belly grow.**

2. **Now exhale hard as if you are blowing out birthday candles.**

3. **Your worries might show up while you are belly breathing. That's okay. Gently focus your attention on your breathing and think about what it feels like to take a deep breath.**

4. **Take more belly breaths for at least two minutes.**

This exercise trains your Laser Focus, because when you're focused on breathing you are not distracted by other things. This exercise is helpful if you have body pains when you wake up in the mornings.

WAKING UP

Do you ever wake up in the morning with a tummy ache? Or as soon as you open your eyes your mind is busy with questions like "What do I have to do today?" If you guessed that this is the feeling of anxiety, then you are right! Some children feel more anxious on Monday mornings because it's a change from the weekend to the weekday. Is that true for you?

When you feel anxious upon waking, it may feel hard to get out of bed. You may start to think of ways you can stay in bed. You may notice aches and pains and even ask your parent if you can stay home. It may be hard to know why you feel aches and pains. Is it anxiety or is it because you might be sick? Let your trusted adult make that decision for you. If they decide that it is anxiety, then the best way to feel better is to actually start your day. Here's why: if you stay home, your anxiety scanner gets a message that waking up and getting ready in the morning is ACTUALLY dangerous. But wait a minute; that seems a bit odd. Is brushing your teeth dangerous? Of course not! Here's your chance to tweak your anxiety scanner so it sends you helpful signals instead of mixed ones. The best thing you can do is to get your morning started even if you feel anxious. You will teach your anxiety scanner that these activities are not dangerous.

Now, let's get your morning started!

TWEAKING YOUR ANXIETY SCANNER

SUPERPOWER: *BEING BRAVE*

Can you pick one thing that makes you feel anxious or uncomfortable in the morning, and, instead of not doing it, can you face it instead? By facing something that may make you feel anxious, you are training your Being Brave superpower. You can do this! Here are some examples that others have tried.

1. **Wake up when my alarm or my parent wakes me up even if I don't feel comfortable.**

2. **Get out of bed on my own even if I have a tummy ache.**

3. **Eat breakfast even if I don't feel like it.**

What are some uncomfortable things that you can try doing in the morning to help reset your anxiety scanner?

DAY OF THE WEEK	UNCOMFORTABLE SITUATION	WAS I ABLE TO DO IT?	HOW UNCOMFORTABLE WAS IT? 1 TO 10 (1=EASY AND 10=VERY UNCOMFORTABLE)
Monday	Eating breakfast even if I don't feel like it	Yes	5

DAY OF THE WEEK	UNCOMFORTABLE SITUATION	WAS I ABLE TO DO IT?	HOW UNCOMFORTABLE WAS IT? 1 TO 10 (1=EASY AND 10=VERY UNCOMFORTABLE)

continued »»

Tweaking Your Anxiety Scanner, *continued*

DAY OF THE WEEK	UNCOMFORTABLE SITUATION	WAS I ABLE TO DO IT?	HOW UNCOMFORTABLE WAS IT? 1 TO 10 (1=EASY AND 10=VERY UNCOMFORTABLE)

It's important to practice these activities every day for at least one week to get the hang of them. It can be the same activity for a week, like eating breakfast every morning, or you can try something different each day. After practicing these uncomfortable things in the morning, did you notice a difference in how you feel? Some people say it's not as uncomfortable anymore. Others say that they just get used to it, and it doesn't bother them as much. How about you?

After practicing these activities for a week I feel _

_ _

_ _

_ _

_ _

GETTING DRESSED AND READY FOR THE DAY

Most people have a morning routine. That means there are things you do every morning to get ready to start your day. Common things to do in the mornings are getting out of bed, getting dressed, brushing your teeth, brushing your hair, eating breakfast, getting your backpack ready, and putting on your shoes and maybe a coat or jacket and hat. Sometimes you have to do these things quickly because you have to get to school on time. But if your worries pop up during your morning routine, it can be hard to focus and remember all the things you have to do.

If you have a tummy ache or headache in the mornings because of anxiety, you may not feel like eating. You might feel picky about your food. You want to eat breakfast, but you don't want to eat the food prepared for you, and you don't know what you would like to eat instead. This is anxiety, too.

When worries show up, it's probably because your mind is wandering. Your mind is trying to figure out what will happen today. The problem is that you are not sure what will actually happen today. You might have an idea of what could happen, but you don't know for sure. Anxiety likes to show up when we feel unsure. You might start noticing those body signals or worries you learned about in chapter 1 when you feel unsure.

Let's tackle how to deal with being unsure by completing the next exercise.

FACING BEING UNSURE

SUPERPOWER: *BEING BRAVE*

Let's try an experiment. What do you think will happen today? In the left-hand column, write down one morning worry. Later, when you get home from school, write down in the middle column what *actually* happened today. In the right-hand column, rate your anxiety about what actually happened. Do this once a day for five days or until the table is filled.

WHAT DO I THINK WILL HAPPEN?	WHAT ACTUALLY HAPPENED?	ON A SCALE FROM 1 TO 10, HOW ANXIOUS DO I FEEL ABOUT WHAT ACTUALLY HAPPENED?
My trusted adult will forget to pick me up from school today	My trusted adult picked me up from school today	1

WHAT DO I THINK WILL HAPPEN?	WHAT ACTUALLY HAPPENED?	ON A SCALE FROM 1 TO 10, HOW ANXIOUS DO I FEEL ABOUT WHAT ACTUALLY HAPPENED?

What are some things that you have learned from the information you wrote down? Did your worries come true? If they didn't come true, the next time you have that worry you can stand up to your worry and say, "That's not true! My trusted adult always picks me up from school." If it did come true, was it as bad as you thought it would be? Did you find a way to solve the problem? If so, you could say to yourself, "Even though my trusted adult was late picking me up, I waited with my friend so I wasn't alone. I had to wait, which I don't like, but I made it home okay."

What have you learned about your worries?

- -

- -

- -

Even though you felt unsure about what was going to happen today, you went on with your day and faced your worry. That's called Being Brave. Nice job and keep up the good work!

LEAVING HOME

Now, you're almost ready to leave for the day. Leaving your home in the morning also means that you will have to be away from your parents for a few hours. That may make you feel anxious. You might have a lot of questions about where they will be, how they will get home, and when they will get home.

When you get anxious, it's easy to focus on the negative. Here's an example that maybe you've seen before. Look at this picture. Would you say that the glass is half empty or half full? Which one is right? If you guessed that both are right, you are correct! They are both right! Now, what if you thought, "Hey, that glass is half empty." How would you feel? Probably not very good. Maybe disappointed? Now, what if you think your glass is half full? You probably would feel better.

This way of thinking is the same with your morning worries. If you focus on being away from your parents, you may feel anxious. But if you focus on going to school, where you will see your teacher and friends, you may feel happier. Both are true, but one makes you feel worse than the other. So, let's use the superpower of Changing Worries to focus on the thoughts that make you feel less anxious. Let's try it!

WHERE'S THE PROOF?

SUPERPOWER: *CHANGING WORRIES*

The superpower of Changing Worries is a way to change big worries to small worries. In this exercise you will have to ask yourself five different questions. Let's review this example together.

MY WORRY: I will give the wrong answer when my teacher calls on me in class.

HOW ANXIOUS DOES THIS WORRY MAKE ME FEEL ON A SCALE FROM 1 TO 10, WITH 1 BEING VERY LOW ANXIETY AND 10 BEING VERY HIGH ANXIETY? My anxiety is a 6.

PROOF THAT MY WORRY IS TRUE	PROOF THAT MY WORRY IS NOT TRUE
I don't really have any proof because I don't know what will happen today	I don't really have any proof because I don't know what will happen today

This table shows that there is no proof on either side, so why believe the worry? If both sides are possible, then why focus on the thought that makes you feel worried? Just like with the glass of water, both can be true but one makes you feel anxious and one does not.

WHAT'S ANOTHER WAY TO LOOK AT THE SITUATION NOW THAT I'VE LOOKED AT THE PROOF? I don't know what will happen today in class. If my teacher calls on me I will do my best.

HOW DO YOU FEEL NOW? My anxiety is a 2.

continued »»

Where's the Proof?, *continued*

Now it's your turn! Fill in the blanks below.

My worry: _

PROOF THAT MY WORRY IS TRUE	PROOF THAT MY WORRY IS NOT TRUE

Now that you've looked at the proof, write down a different way you could look at the situation.

_ _

_ _

_ _

_ _

_ _

How do you feel now? _

MY PLAN
TO BE BRAVE IN
THE MORNINGS

You've learned a lot about how anxiety can appear first thing in the morning and how it may affect you. You've done an amazing job learning about your morning worries and what to do when they pop up. You practiced how to release tension in your body. You used courage to face things that make you anxious. You learned how to change big worries to small ones.

Now let's think about which exercises or superpowers were most helpful to you. Go back and read your answers from the exercises in this chapter. You could ask a trusted adult about which ones they think helped you. Usually, a sign that a superpower worked is if you were able to do something you couldn't do before. For example, you couldn't eat breakfast because your tummy hurt, but now you can. Or if it took you a long time to get out of bed but now it's much easier. The next two exercises will help you figure out which superpowers helped you the most. Keep up the good work!

MY FAVORITE MORNING SUPERPOWERS

SUPERPOWER: ....

Think about the different superpowers you learned in this chapter and the exercises you completed to practice them. You learned the superpower of Laser Focus by relaxing your muscles and taking belly breaths. You also learned the superpower of Changing Worries using the Where's the Proof? exercise (page 33). And you practiced Being Brave by facing your discomfort and uncertainty. Pick the superpowers you found most helpful and draw what they look like to you.

MY MORNING ACTION PLAN

SUPERPOWER: *BEING BRAVE*

It's time to make a morning action plan. With a plan, you will be prepared when worries show up in the morning. Starting from the left, in the Situation column, write down what was happening when your worries showed up. In the My Worry column, write down what worries you in the morning. In the My Exercise column, write down the name of one of your favorite exercises to deal with those worries. Finally, in the My Superpower column, write down which superpower that exercise belongs to. Let's complete one together.

SITUATION	MY WORRY	MY EXERCISE	MY SUPERPOWER
When brushing my teeth	My classmate will be mean to me	Where's the Proof?	Changing Worries

Now you fill in the rest!

SITUATION	MY WORRY	MY EXERCISE	MY SUPERPOWER

continued »»

My Morning Action Plan, *continued*

SITUATION	MY WORRY	MY EXERCISE	MY SUPERPOWER

CHAPTER 3

Me at School

HOW DO I FEEL AT SCHOOL?

The feeling of anxiety can show up on your way to school or during your school day. The reason may not be clear. It could be because you are feeling unsure about what may happen at school that day, or maybe it's your anxiety scanner sending you wrong messages. Remember what happens when you feel unsure? That's right! Anxiety shows up. If your anxiety scanner thinks it detects a threat, it will send you messages in the shape of worries like "Beware! Something bad might happen at school." Worries start popping up like popcorn and then those worries could make you feel more anxious.

You may be tempted to fix feeling anxious at school through avoidance. For example, maybe you avoid talking to your teacher or skip some answers on a class assignment to avoid anxiety. You also may be tempted to avoid feeling anxious by trying to be perfect. You'd have to work extremely hard to not make a single mistake at school. The problem with these strategies is that they don't last for long. If you avoid talking to your teacher when you need help or if you avoid completing schoolwork, then you won't learn the material. If you overdo it and aim for perfection, you will put too much pressure on yourself and miss out on having fun in school. This chapter will give you new strategies to help you face anxiety at school in a healthy way.

THINGS I WORRY ABOUT AT SCHOOL

SUPERPOWER: *BEING BRAVE*

Let's learn what worries you at school. By using your Being Brave superpower, you can be open and honest about the things you're afraid of.

1. **In the list of Things I Worry About at School, circle what makes you feel anxious at school.**

2. **Next, take a look at the items you circled and rate how anxious each one makes you from 1 to 10, with 1 being the least anxious and 10 being the most anxious.**

3. **Finally, put the worries you rated in order from most anxiety provoking to least anxiety provoking.**

THINGS I WORRY ABOUT AT SCHOOL	RATING
Being late	- - - - - - - -
Speaking in class	- - - - - - - -
Presenting in front of class	- - - - - - - -
Being called on by the teacher	- - - - - - - -
Asking the teacher a question	- - - - - - - -
Having to work in a group	- - - - - - - -
Making a mistake	- - - - - - - -

Failing at an assignment   - - - - - - - -

Teacher being upset with me   - - - - - - - -

Making friends   - - - - - - - -

Classmates being mean to me   - - - - - - - -

Classmates who don't like me   - - - - - - - -

Not knowing how to do the class assignment   - - - - - - - -

Falling in gym class   - - - - - - - -

Not having anyone to play with at recess   - - - - - - - -

Not knowing who to sit with at lunch   - - - - - - - -

Eating lunch in front of others   - - - - - - - -

Using the school bathroom   - - - - - - - -

Having a tummy ache or headache at school   - - - - - - - -

Getting sick at school   - - - - - - - -

Being picked up after school   - - - - - - - -

Getting in trouble at school   - - - - - - - -

Forgetting something at home   - - - - - - - -

Taking a quiz or a test   - - - - - - - -

continued »»

Things I Worry About at School, *continued*

Other _

Rank your worries from most anxiety provoking to least anxiety provoking:

1. _

2. _

3. _

4. _

5. _

FACING DISCOMFORT

SUPERPOWER: *BEING BRAVE*

Feeling uncomfortable is not fun, so facing uncomfortable situations at school may feel really scary. But don't give up! Here is an exercise that can help you practice facing some discomfort so you can work up to facing uncomfortable situations at school. Try this at home on a weekend.

Let's pretend that you are getting ready to go to school. You've gotten dressed and walk to the bathroom to brush your teeth, but your left sock slides down to your heel. You stop and fix it. By the time you walk to the kitchen and sit down for breakfast, your sock has slid down three more times! How annoying! You have a choice. You can spend the rest of the day fixing your sock every few minutes, or you can just leave it bunched up in the middle of your foot. What would happen if you leave your sock alone? It would feel uncomfortable at first, but as the day goes on it wouldn't feel as annoying as it did in the morning. Or maybe it still feels annoying, but you would be able to go on with your day and focus on things that were more fun or important to you.

That's what the exercise of Tweaking Your Anxiety Scanner (page 26) is asking you to do. By using your Being Brave superpower, can you do something even if it makes you uncomfortable because that thing is important to you or a lot of fun? For example, can you ask others to play at recess even if you don't know if they want to play with you? The outcome could be that you make new friends and have fun! That's worth facing something uncomfortable.

So as a way to practice feeling uncomfortable, let's see how long and how much you can get done when a sock is stuck around the arch of your foot.

continued »»

Facing Discomfort, *continued*

After five minutes, how did you feel walking around and going about your day with

your sock around your foot? _

How strongly did you feel that way? _

After 10 minutes, how did you feel walking around and going about your day with

your sock around your foot? _

How strongly did you feel that way? _

After 15 minutes, how did you feel walking around and going about your day with

your sock around your foot? _

How strongly did you feel that way? _

If you were able to keep your sock down for longer than 15 minutes, that is AMAZING! You are working so hard! If you weren't able to resist the need to fix the sock, go back and see if you can try the exercise again.

SUPERHERO SLOGANS

SUPERPOWER: *BEING BRAVE*

Sometimes saying encouraging things to yourself can help you face the day. Here are some superhero slogans that can help you.

"I am brave and I can do this!"

"I may feel anxious, but I can face whatever comes my way."

"I know how to handle my anxiety."

"I did this before, and I can do it again."

"It might feel hard, but I will do my best."

Can you think of one or two more?

1. _____

2. _____

GETTING SETTLED AT SCHOOL

Changing subjects from math to spelling in class or going from sitting at your desk to sitting on the reading carpet are all examples of "transitions." Transitions are when things change from one subject or place to another. Some people get really anxious during transitions. Take a minute to think if that may be true for you.

When there is a change, the anxiety scanner starts to scan for possible danger. That's when a lot of "what-ifs" pop up as well, such as, "What if I don't get to sit next to my friend?" These worries are meant to help you predict a problem and fix it before it happens. But sometimes they just make you feel anxious instead of helping.

People who feel anxious during transitions are usually afraid of the unknown. A change means that something new or different will happen, and with that change comes a lot of unknown things. Like transitioning from your desk to the reading carpet. "What will we read?" "Where should I sit?"

During a transition time, try to focus on one step at a time. If you are going from your class to recess, think of the very next step you should take. Is it clearing your desk? Don't let your thoughts run away too fast and far ahead. If you find that your thoughts are already zoomed ahead to recess, gently bring them back to the classroom. Remember, you are still in the classroom getting ready to leave. Now, let's learn how to grow your Laser Focus.

BEING PRESENT

SUPERPOWER: *LASER FOCUS*

This superpower will teach you how to have Laser Focus on the present so that your worries don't carry you away into the future. To do this you will need your five senses: sight, touch, taste, sound, and smell.

To activate Laser Focus, name one thing in each sense category that is happening right now. If you get distracted by a worry, that's okay. Gently bring your mind back to your senses. Let's do one together.

Right now I see my desk.

Right now I feel the hard surface of my desk.

Right now I taste the snack I ate earlier.

Right now I hear the other kids clearing their desks.

Right now I smell the outside air coming in from the open windows.

Now you try!

Right now I see _____

Right now I feel _____

Right now I taste _____

Right now I hear _____

Right now I smell _____

continued »»

Being Present, *continued*

How do you feel now that you practiced your Laser Focus superpower with your five senses? Does anything feel different? _____

_____

_____

_____

_____

_____

_____

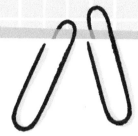

CLASSES AND SCHOOLWORK

Feeling anxious in class can get in the way of learning. When you have lots of worries bouncing around in your head, it can be hard to focus on what the teacher is saying. It's so easy to get distracted by the "what-ifs"!

If you are working on an assignment in class, anxiety can make you worried about making a mistake or doubt your answers. If you are afraid of making a mistake, it may take you a very long time trying to find the perfect answer before you write it down. You might read, reread, erase, and rewrite in class to avoid a mistake. You might double- or triple-check your answers. All of this can be exhausting!

If you are taking a quiz or a test, your mind can go blank from feeling anxious. Remember fight, flight, or freeze? Your mind going blank is the same as freezing. Or, your worries start popping up and slow down your thinking and make it hard to finish on time. Anxiety can make you doubt the answers you write down on your quiz or test, making it hard to decide whether you are finished.

The good news is that you have already learned the basics on how to manage feeling anxious in the classroom. Facing Discomfort (page 45) could work here, or you can try the next exercise.

GOOD ENOUGH PLAN

SUPERPOWER: *BEING BRAVE*

What are some things that you do to give the perfect answer? Do you take a long time to read and reread? Do you spend too much time writing and rewriting your answers? Do you double-, triple-, or quadruple-check your answers? If so, it's time to learn when your answers are "good enough."

Your Good Enough Plan should target either limiting how much time you spend on an assignment or limiting how many times you redo or reread your assignment.

My Good Enough Plan

I agree to read or write no more than twice when I am in class. Even if I really want to fix it, I will stick to reading a passage no more than twice, and writing and rewriting a sentence no more than twice.

Let's keep track of what you try to change and how anxious it makes you feel with your Good Enough Plan. Here's an example:

WHAT ACTION DID I TRY TO CHANGE?	HOW ANXIOUS DID IT MAKE ME FEEL? (1=LOW ANXIETY TO 10=HIGH ANXIETY)
Writing and rewriting	4

Now it's your turn. Try one new action to change every day for one week and write it down in this chart.

WHAT ACTION DID I TRY TO CHANGE?	HOW ANXIOUS DID IT MAKE ME FEEL? (1=LOW ANXIETY TO 10=HIGH ANXIETY)

After you've tried this for a week, how do you feel? _

_ _

_ _

FRIENDS AND FREE TIME

When you are learning in class, there are certain class rules you have to follow. You know that you have to listen to the teacher. You have to sit in your seat. If you want to speak, you have to raise your hand. You can't distract the other students. You have to take turns and so on.

But there are other times in the day when there aren't as many rules, like during recess or lunchtime. Sometimes not having as many rules can spike anxiety in a person because it's not really clear how you should act. It's not really clear who you should sit next to at lunch, what you should do at recess, or what you should talk about with your classmates. Whenever something is not clear, that's when anxiety can show up. Take a minute and see if that may be true for you.

If anxiety shows up during free time, you may want to avoid those times. You may decide to stay in the classroom instead of going outside to play with others during recess. Or if recess is inside, you might keep to yourself instead of playing with others. You might skip lunch by going to the nurse's office. You have already learned that staying away from situations that make you feel uncomfortable teaches your anxiety scanner that those situations are dangerous. Use the superpower of Being Brave by revisiting the Tweaking Your Anxiety Scanner (page 26) or Facing Being Unsure (page 30) exercises to stay in those uncomfortable situations. The next exercise can help, too!

WHAT'S THE WORST THAT COULD HAPPEN?

SUPERPOWER: *CHANGING WORRIES*

This superpower will teach you how to change your worries from big to small. First, take a moment to identify your worry. Did you find it? Okay. Now, ask yourself, "What's the worst that could happen?" "What's the best that could happen?" And finally, "What's something in between that could happen?" Let's do one together.

MY WORRY: I don't know who to play with at recess.

ON A SCALE FROM 1 TO 10, WHERE 1 IS LOW ANXIETY AND 10 IS HIGH ANXIETY, HOW ANXIOUS DOES THIS WORRY MAKE YOU FEEL? 5

WHAT'S THE WORST THAT COULD HAPPEN? I will play by myself.

WHAT'S THE BEST THAT COULD HAPPEN? I will find several friends to play with.

WHAT'S SOMETHING IN BETWEEN THAT COULD HAPPEN? I will find one friend to play with.

HOW DO I FEEL IF I BELIEVE THE SOMETHING-IN-BETWEEN ANSWER?
My anxiety went from a 5 to a 2.

Now, it's your turn!

continued »»

What's the Worst That Could Happen?, *continued*

MY WORRY IS: _____

On a scale from 1 to 10, where 1 is low anxiety and 10 is high anxiety, how anxious does this worry make you feel? _____

What's the worst that could happen? _____

What's the best that could happen? _____

What's something in between that could happen? _____

How do I feel if I believe the something-in-between answer? _____

MY PLAN TO BE BRAVE AT SCHOOL

You've learned a lot about when anxiety can show up during your school day and why that may be true for you. You learned how to use Laser Focus to get past things that feel uncomfortable. You practiced how to know when your homework is good enough. You learned how to focus on the present to avoid running away with anxiety.

Go back and review your answers from the exercises in this chapter. Maybe ask a trusted adult about which ones they think helped you. Usually a sign that a superpower worked is if you were able to do something you had a hard time doing. For example, did you volunteer to help your teacher or spend less time looking for the perfect answer? Let's make a plan to practice these for the next week so that you can strengthen these superpowers and keep your anxiety from getting in the way of having fun!

The next two exercises will also help with figuring out which exercises were helpful to you. Once you have a final list of superpowers, then you can plan to use them at school this week. Keep up the good work!

MY FAVORITE SCHOOL SUPERPOWERS

SUPERPOWER: ....

Think about the different superpowers you learned in this chapter and the exercises you completed to practice them. You learned so many ways to face feeling anxious, from rooting for yourself to facing being uncomfortable and limiting how much you redo things in class. You also learned how to grow Laser Focus and change big worries to small worries. A lot of the superpowers that ask you to face your anxiety will require practice. So after you've practiced them, did you notice any change in how you feel? Maybe those situations aren't as uncomfortable anymore. Do you feel more confident at school? Maybe you are doing more things at school or the worries just don't bother you as much. Those are all good signs that facing being uncomfortable has worked. Now your anxiety scanner can continue being helpful.

Pick the superpowers you found most helpful and draw something fun from them.

MY SCHOOLTIME ACTION PLAN

SUPERPOWER: *BEING BRAVE*

It's time to make a schooltime action plan. With a plan, you will be prepared when worries show up during school. Starting from the left, in the Situation column, write down what was happening when your worries showed up. In the My Worry column, write down what worries you while at school. In the My Exercise column, write down the name of one of your favorite exercises to deal with those worries. Finally, in the My Superpower column, write down which superpower that exercise belongs to. Let's complete one together.

SITUATION	MY WORRY	MY EXERCISE	MY SUPERPOWER
In class	I may make a mistake	What's the Worst That Could Happen?	Changing Worries

Now you fill in the rest!

SITUATION	MY WORRY	MY EXERCISE	MY SUPERPOWER

continued »»

My Schooltime Action Plan, *continued*

SITUATION	MY WORRY	MY EXERCISE	MY SUPERPOWER

Me After School

HOW DO I FEEL AFTER SCHOOL?

The end of the school day is another time of transition. As we discussed in chapter 3, a transition is when there is a change coming up. What that after-school change is for you may depend on the day of the week.

There are lots of fun things to do after school. Sometimes it's an after-school activity or program. Maybe you get to play with your friends or family members. Or sometimes you may go straight home. How you travel from school to an after-school activity or your friend's house may not always be the same, either. Your parent may take you one day and then the next week it's your friend's parent that takes you. Sometimes you might need to take a bus, ride your bike, or just walk.

Because this is a time of change, that feeling of being unsure can show up, which means anxiety and worries can pop up as well. The four superpowers that you have learned about can all help in these situations.

In this chapter, we will go over some useful exercises to help you tap into your superpowers and deal with worries and anxiety that occur when the school day is over. The next exercise will help you learn which after-school situations may make you feel anxious. Use your Being Brave superpower to figure out which situations make you anxious, and you will learn a new set of superpowers to deal with those anxious moments.

THINGS I WORRY ABOUT AFTER SCHOOL

SUPERPOWER: *BEING BRAVE*

Let's learn what worries you after school. By using your Being Brave superpower, you can be open and honest about the things you're afraid of.

1. **In the list of Things I Worry about after School, circle what makes you feel anxious after school.**

2. **Next, take a look at the items you circled and rate how anxious each one makes you from 1 to 10, with 1 being the least anxious and 10 being the most anxious.**

3. **Finally, put the worries you rated in order from most anxiety provoking to least anxiety provoking.**

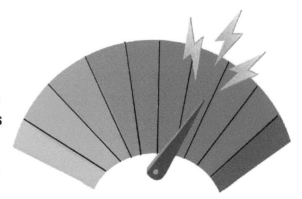

THINGS I WORRY ABOUT AFTER SCHOOL	RATING
Who will pick me up after school	- - - - - - - -
How will I get to my after-school destination	- - - - - - - -
What if I don't like my after-school snack	- - - - - - - -
Being late to my after-school activity	- - - - - - - -
Making a mistake at practice	- - - - - - - -
Losing a sports game	- - - - - - - -

Disappointing my coach — — — — — — —

Misplacing my homework — — — — — — —

Having enough time to do my homework — — — — — — —

Not understanding my homework — — — — — — —

Studying for a quiz or test — — — — — — —

Working on a long-term project — — — — — — —

Not knowing who will help me with my homework — — — — — — —

Not liking my dinner — — — — — — —

Not having enough free time — — — — — — —

Falling asleep — — — — — — —

Staying asleep — — — — — — —

Other _ — — — — — — —

Rank your worries from most anxiety provoking
to least anxiety provoking:

1. _

2. _

3. _

4. _

5. _

MINDFUL BUBBLES

SUPERPOWER: *GETTING UNSTUCK*

If you ever feel like your worries get "stuck" in your brain, this exercise will help. You will learn to watch your worries. Why would you want to watch your worries, you ask? Watching your worries helps them get "unstuck" from your brain. If you are not distracted by your worries, then that means you are more likely to do things you like to do instead of worrying. Let's try it.

1. Imagine you are blowing bubbles. What do the bubbles look like? Some bubbles are so big that you can fit in them, and others are teeny tiny. Some bubbles pop immediately, and others linger for a while.

2. Now imagine putting a worry you have into a bubble and watching it float away. The bubble may come back toward you, or it may go up or down, and that's okay. Other bubbles may pop immediately or linger for a while and that's okay, too. Don't touch the bubbles or try to change where they are going, just watch what the bubbles do.

3. Now do this with the next worry you have. Think of your worries as bubbles. Imagine putting a worry in a bubble. Notice how it floats! Now imagine giving it a big, breathy blow to send it away. Do this again when you feel another worry pop up. You don't have to listen to what the worry says; instead, you can watch the worry with the same curiosity you have when you blow real bubbles.

How do you feel after doing this exercise? What happened to your thoughts?

Now you try. Write a worry in each bubble below. Next time you are distracted by a worry, try to imagine this exercise.

FEARLESS WORDS

SUPERPOWER: *GETTING UNSTUCK*

Let's strengthen your superpower of Getting Unstuck from your worries so that they don't scare you. Did you know that if you repeat a word or a sentence really quickly over and over again, it starts to lose its meaning? It starts to sound funny! It's hard to be afraid of the word "monstermonstermonstermonstermonster," and that can make it less scary for you. Let's give it a try! For 30 seconds say the word "milk" over and over again as fast as you can. You can do this with a trusted adult and see who can say it the fastest!

Now answer the following questions:

What did the word sound like? _

How do you feel after doing that? _

Now try repeating one of your own worries, like "lotsofhomeworklotsofhomework." How did that make you feel?

_ _

AFTER-SCHOOL ACTIVITIES

Think about the after-school activities that you do. If you meet with a tutor, you will practice doing things that may be hard for you. Doing things that are hard usually means that you are doing something that makes you feel uncomfortable. Some people try to avoid feeling uncomfortable, such as not going to tutoring, but in the end that makes the problem worse because they don't learn what they need to.

If you go to an after-school activity, like a sports practice, you might also have to practice doing something that is hard. You might start comparing yourself to your teammates. If you have a sports game, you might worry about making a mistake and about winning. You might also worry about what your coach is thinking.

Let's consider the idea that some things can be worth being uncomfortable for. For example, if you care about doing well in school, it may be worth being uncomfortable during tutoring so that later you can be proud of your hard work. What if you went to practice feeling uncomfortable? What if you are brave enough to let those uncomfortable feelings just be there without trying to get rid of them?

Superpowers that you have already learned can help you be brave during these after-school activities. You can practice the superpower of Being Brave through exercises like Facing Being Unsure (page 30) and Tweaking Your Anxiety Scanner (page 26). These exercises can help if you are feeling anxious after school. Or you can try the next exercise.

PLAYING PRETEND

SUPERPOWER: *BEING BRAVE*

Think of the after-school activities that make you feel uncomfortable. Are there some that you stopped doing? If so, this exercise is for you.

Think of what it would be like to attend that after-school activity if you didn't feel anxious. Would you go? Would you do anything differently there? Now if you said yes, then the next time the activity is scheduled, can you go and pretend as if you weren't feeling anxious? What would you do differently if you weren't anxious?

Write or draw what happened when you pretended like you weren't anxious during your after-school activity.

Can you keep going to the after-school activity even if you felt anxious?

HOMEWORK AND STUDYING

Doing homework after school can be a tricky time. Sometimes homework can be easy. You finish it very quickly and you can go play and have fun. Other times homework can be hard and you may need some help. Sometimes homework takes a long time. If a certain subject is hard for you, it's easy to get overwhelmed by worries. Some people deal with difficult homework by avoiding it until bedtime. That's usually not a helpful strategy, because they'll be tired around bedtime, and it will make doing homework even harder.

Some people put a lot of pressure on themselves because they want their homework or project to be perfect. They might fear that if the homework isn't perfect they may get a bad grade or the teacher will be "mad" at them.

Studying for a test or a quiz may be tricky, too. You might doubt yourself when studying, which makes it hard to tell if you are done. So you spend more time than needed on studying just to make sure you didn't miss anything. But this extra studying may lead to more anxiety. You could miss out on doing other things that you enjoy. It could put you in a bad mood for the rest of the evening because you are worrying about the quiz. Other people may decide that studying is too hard and give up. That's not a helpful way of studying, either, because you don't learn what you need to.

Don't fall into a worry pit! Try this next exercise to help you deal with worries during homework time.

WORRY TIME

SUPERPOWER: *CHANGING WORRIES*

This is a useful exercise to try if you have a lot of worries about homework and studying.

Find a sheet of paper and a pencil to write with or ask a grown-up to borrow a device to record your voice. For no more than 10 minutes, write, draw, or say all the worries that you have about homework and school. If you don't feel like writing, you can tell your worries to a trusted adult instead who will listen, or they can write down or record you with a phone or computer.

The reason why this works is because writing down or saying our worries out loud can make them feel less scary. Doing this activity can help us think of a way to change the shape of those worries. Getting your worries out can help you focus on homework later. It is best if you set a regular time every day to worry for no more than 10 minutes.

If you have a homework worry during the day, save it for your after-school worry time.

Now you try. Draw your homework and school worries here.

continued »»

Worry Time, *continued*

Write or tell your homework and schoolwork worries for no more than 10 minutes. How do you feel afterward?

DINNERTIME

Imagine you are having fun playing a game, and all of a sudden you hear, "Dinner!" This is another transition time. You might not want to stop what you are doing because you are having fun.

Perhaps you are very focused on doing your homework or studying. This may also make it difficult to stop what you are doing and join your family for dinner.

If you are already feeling anxious, you may not feel hungry. Your stomach might feel tight. When you are feeling anxious, some things about food may bother you. Sometimes people don't like the texture, smell, color, or temperature of the food they are served. Think about it for a minute and see if that may be true for you.

Even if you may not feel hungry for dinner, your stomach could still be empty. You may not be getting signals from your tummy that it would like to get some food. However, eating at dinnertime can actually help you with feeling less anxious. It's easier to deal with worries and anxiety when your body gets the nutrients it needs.

Your Laser Focus superpower can be super helpful here. Can you tap into your five senses and see if you can take a bite of dinner? The Belly Breathing (page 24) and Tension Buster (page 23) exercises can be helpful, too, if your stomach feels like it can't take any food. These two exercises can help relax your muscles, which may make it easier to eat.

You can also try this next exercise!

MINDFUL BUTTERFLY

SUPERPOWER: *GETTING UNSTUCK*

If you don't feel hungry around dinnertime, give this exercise a try. You may need a parent to read the exercise out loud to you so you can practice. This exercise will help you focus your attention on your body, which can help you notice different sensations, such as hunger.

1. Lay down and close your eyes. Take a deep belly breath.

2. Pretend that a butterfly lands on your shoulder. Take a minute to notice what you feel in your shoulder. Now imagine the butterfly flying to your other shoulder. What do you feel there? Take a few seconds to notice different sensations in your shoulders.

3. Take a deep belly breath. The butterfly lands on your nose. What do you feel there? Do you notice any tension in your face?

4. Now take a belly breath again. The butterfly lands on your tummy. What do you notice there?

5. Take another belly breath. The butterfly leaves your tummy and lands on your leg. What do you notice there? Any twitching or tension?

6. The butterfly lands on your other leg. What do you feel there?

7. Take a final belly breath. Breathe in and out. Now slowly count backward from three to one. Three, two, one. You can open your eyes.

What sensations do you notice now that this exercise is done?

MY PLAN TO BE BRAVE AFTER SCHOOL

You've learned a lot about when anxiety can show up after school and why that may be true for you. You practiced how to release your worries that get stuck in your brain. You learned how to give your mind some worry time to let all the worries out. You practiced a mindfulness exercise to relax your whole body.

Go back and review your answers from the exercises in this chapter. Maybe ask a trusted adult about which ones they think helped you. Usually a sign that a superpower worked is if you were able to do something you had a hard time doing. For example, did you start your homework earlier or maybe you ate more than what you usually eat at dinner? Let's make a plan to practice these for the next week so that you can strengthen these superpowers and keep your anxiety from getting in the way of having fun and learning!

The next two exercises will also help with figuring out which exercises are your best helpers. Once you have a final list of superpowers, then you can plan to use them after school this week. Keep up the good work!

MY FAVORITE AFTER-SCHOOL SUPERPOWERS

SUPERPOWER: --------------------

Think about the different superpowers you learned in this chapter and the exercises you completed to practice them. In this chapter you learned so many ways to face feeling anxious: you learned how to watch your worries and how to listen to your body. A lot of the superpowers will require practice. So after you've practiced them, did you notice any change in how you feel? Maybe those situations aren't as uncomfortable anymore? Maybe you are doing more things after school or the worries just don't bother you as much? Those are all good signs that facing being uncomfortable has worked and has recalibrated your anxiety scanner so that it can continue being helpful. Pick the superpowers you found most helpful and draw them.

MY AFTER-SCHOOL ACTION PLAN

SUPERPOWER: *BEING BRAVE*

It's time to make an after-school action plan. With a plan, you will be prepared when worries show up after school. Starting from the left, in the Situation column, write down what was happening when your worries showed up. In the My Worry column, write down what worries you after school. In the My Exercise column, write down the name of one of your favorite exercises to deal with those worries. Finally, in the My Superpower column, write down which superpower that exercise belongs to. Let's complete one together.

SITUATION	MY WORRY	MY EXERCISE	MY SUPERPOWER
Doing my homework	What if I'm doing this wrong?	Worry Time	Being Brave

Now you fill in the rest!

continued »»

My After-School Action Plan, *continued*

SITUATION	MY WORRY	MY EXERCISE	MY SUPERPOWER

CHAPTER 5

Me at Bedtime

HOW DO I FEEL AT BEDTIME?

You've had a fun day of school and after-school activities. Through-out the day you probably felt a lot of different feelings like excitement, joy, annoyance, calmness, boredom, and so on. For some people, the feeling of anxiety only shows up at bedtime. Take a moment and see if some of those anxiety signals we talked about in chapter 1 are present at bedtime.

Worries pop up at bedtime because your mind is not as distracted by activities. Your mind is free to wander and wonder. You may have a lot of questions or worries that you want to talk about with your parent. Your worries might get stuck in your head and make it hard to fall asleep.

Sometimes bedtime worries are about what happened earlier that day. Your mind may go back and review the day checking for mistakes. Other bedtime worries are about the future, like wondering what will happen tomorrow at or after school.

This chapter will go over ways to deal with bedtime worries. In the meantime, while you learn new exercises to strengthen your superpow-ers, you can always practice some you've already learned. Maybe you can try Tension Buster (page 23), What's the Worst That Could Happen? (page 55), or Mindful Bubbles (page 66). The following exercises can be helpful, too.

THINGS I WORRY ABOUT AT BEDTIME

SUPERPOWER: *BEING BRAVE*

Let's learn which worries you might have at bedtime. By using your Being Brave superpower, you can be open and honest about the things you're afraid of.

1. **In the list of Things I Worry About at Bedtime, circle what makes you anxious at bedtime.**

2. **Next, take a look at the items you circled and rate how anxious each one makes you from 1 to 10, with 1 being the least anxious and 10 being the most anxious.**

3. **Finally, put the worries you rated in order from most anxiety provoking to least anxiety provoking.**

THINGS I WORRY ABOUT AT BEDTIME	RATING
Monsters under the bed or in the closet	- - - - - - - -
The dark	- - - - - - - -
Something bad happening at night	- - - - - - - -
Someone breaking in	- - - - - - - -
Sleeping alone	- - - - - - - -
Being away from my parents	- - - - - - - -
The feeling of falling asleep	- - - - - - - -

Falling asleep   - - - - - - - -

Waking up in the middle of the night   - - - - - - - -

Having an accident in my bed   - - - - - - - -

What will happen the next day?   - - - - - - - -

Worries about offending someone earlier that day   - - - - - - - -

Worries about making a mistake earlier in the day   - - - - - - - -

Worries about something I did earlier in the day   - - - - - - - -

Worries about something happening tomorrow   - - - - - - - -

Homework   - - - - - - - -

Quiz   - - - - - - - -

Getting up in the morning   - - - - - - - -

Getting to school the next day   - - - - - - - -

Other: _   - - - - - - - -

Rank your worries from most anxiety provoking to least anxiety provoking:

1. _

2. _

3. _

4. _

5. _

SLEEP TIPS

SUPERPOWER: *LASER FOCUS*

Did you know that when you are able to get a good night's sleep, you build energy back up? It's true! And having energy to tackle your anxiety is always a good thing.

Take a look at these 5 tips that can help you sleep better:

1. **Have a cool temperature in your room. We sleep better in a cooler room.**

2. **Milk has a special ingredient that can make you feel sleepy. So, if you can drink milk, try some before bed. Ask a trusted adult before you do.**

3. **Have the same bedtime every night and the same wake-up time.**

4. **Put screens away at least 30 minutes before bedtime to help prepare your brain to fall asleep.**

5. **Stay away from sugary or caffeinated drinks in the evenings.**

Which tip seems easiest for you to follow? Write it down here.

- -

Now it's time to challenge yourself to be brave and make decisions that may not always be the easiest ones to make. Try a different tip from the list each night this week. Then come back and write down the three tips that became your favorite.

My favorite sleep tips are:

WATCHING CLOUDS

SUPERPOWER: *GETTING UNSTUCK*

This superpower will help you get your bedtime worries unstuck. If you are not distracted by your worries, then that means you are more likely to fall asleep instead of worrying. This is similar to the Mindful Bubbles exercise (page 66) and will help you "watch" your worries so that you can fall asleep. Let's try it.

You can keep your eyes open or closed for this exercise, whatever makes you comfortable. Imagine you are staring up at the blue sky with lots of clouds. Some clouds are round, others remind you of animal shapes, while some others look like whipped cream. Some clouds can join together and form a really big cloud, and others kind of melt into the sky. What other cloud shapes do you see? Now place each worry you have on a cloud. Watch as the cloud drifts away with your worry. If your worry comes back, that's okay, just put it back on a cloud.

Write down two worries you have at night and put them on the clouds below.

GETTING READY FOR BED

Getting ready for bed is another transition time. You have to stop what you are doing, which may be hard because you are having a good time, and start getting ready for bed. You might have a lot of energy, and you may just not feel sleepy yet, so when your parent says it's time to brush your teeth you might say, "Can I have five more minutes?" You might have worries about being able to fall asleep, so you put off getting ready for bed.

When getting ready for bed, you probably brush your teeth and change into your pajamas. What are some other things you do when you get ready for bed?

If your worries pop up during this time, you could get distracted from getting ready for bed, like brushing your teeth really slowly because your mind is stuck on worries. Or if your worries show up while you are in bed, you might take a long time putting your pajamas on. Some people get easily distracted by little things as a way of delaying bedtime. Like, "I wonder where my favorite LEGO set is? Mom! Do you know where my favorite LEGO set is?"

If this is true for you, try your Changing Worries superpower with the Where's the Proof? (page 33) exercise to deal with worries when you are getting ready for bed. The next exercise can help, too.

BEDTIME FOCUS

SUPERPOWER: *LASER FOCUS*

You practiced your Laser Focus superpower for schooltime in chapter 3. This time let's use Laser Focus when getting ready for bed. Let's see how tapping into this superpower will help clear your worries.

You can activate bedtime laser focus with any of your bedtime tasks. Here's an example of how to do it while you are brushing your teeth.

WHAT DO I SEE? I see a mirror, sink, faucet, toothpaste, and a white bathroom wall.

WHAT DO I HEAR? I hear the sound of my toothbrush brushing my teeth. I hear the sound of me spitting the toothpaste out of my mouth. I hear the sound of water running.

WHAT DO I TASTE? My fruity toothpaste.

WHAT DO I FEEL? The bristles of my toothbrush against my teeth and inside my cheek. I feel bubbles forming in my mouth. I feel toothpaste in my mouth.

WHAT DO I SMELL? The fruity smell of my toothpaste and soap.

Now you try it!

What do I see? _____

What do I hear? _____

What do I taste? _

What do I feel? _

What do I smell? _

Did you notice your focus improve? Sometimes putting our whole focus on one thing at a time can make us feel calmer. Now write down how you feel:

_ _

_ _

BEDTIME TUCK-IN

A lot of kids have a bedtime routine like reading a bedtime story, singing a song, or being tucked in by your parents. Some kids need their parent to say goodnight a certain way in order for them to fall asleep.

Your bedtime routine can help you feel relaxed and sleepy. But if anxiety shows up at night, sometimes this routine isn't enough. It may be hard to separate from your parent at night because when they are around you don't feel anxious. But when they start to leave, your anxiety may start showing up and lots of worry thoughts may keep you awake. You might ask your parent a lot of worry questions like "Will you take me to school tomorrow?", even though you know your parent always takes you to school. You may try to extend bedtime tuck-in by asking for one more bedtime story or for one more song. Other kids ask their parent to bring lots of things into their room like water, a snack, or a different stuffed animal, to help them fall asleep.

Sleep is important to help you grow and be healthy. That means it's important to stick to your bedtime routine and not extend it even though you really want to. Some useful superpowers you can already use include Changing Worries using the Superhero Slogans (page 47) exercise and Getting Unstuck from your worries through the Fearless Words (page 68) exercise.

BEDTIME READING

SUPERPOWER: *LASER FOCUS*

You can try this exercise to help you feel sleepy when you are being tucked in. Instead of reading a book you are interested in, read a book that you find boring. Seriously! What happens when you read a book you think is boring? You start yawning, right? Exactly! Sometimes reading a story that you are not interested in can help you fall asleep. Ask your parent to help you find a book that you think is dull. Now, record what that book was and how it made you feel!

Name of book: _____

How do you feel after reading this book? _____

_____

SLEEPING TIME

You're all tucked in, and it's time to close your eyes and fall asleep. But worries don't have a bedtime. In fact, when it's quiet and you are lying in bed, that's exactly when they may show up. Worries are free to run wild with your imagination. "What's that dark thing on the floor?" "What was that sound?" "What if I do something wrong tomorrow?" This makes it really hard to relax and fall asleep.

It can be hard to turn off those worries. Kids try different things to fall back asleep, like go to their parents' room and ask to sleep in their bed. Parents may choose to let them, or tell them to go back to their own bed. This may happen several times at night. Other kids feel like they have to go to the bathroom but then once they get there they can't. So they may go back and forth between their bed and the bathroom several times at night. If this is true for you, then you must be very tired in the morning!

When you don't sleep through the night, it may be extra hard to get up in the morning. It may even mean you have worries first thing in the morning. That sounds exhausting!

Thankfully, you already have some superpowers you can try like Laser Focus with Belly Breathing (page 24) or your Bedtime Reading to fall asleep. You can also try the next exercise.

MY NIGHTTIME THOUGHTS AND WORRIES

SUPERPOWER: *GETTING UNSTUCK*

If you are having a hard time falling asleep because your worries are keeping you awake, try to write or draw them below. That way you can get them out of your mind and clear your head of worries.

1. _____

2. _____

3. _____

4. _____

5. _____

MY PLAN TO BE BRAVE AT BEDTIME

You've learned about how anxiety and worries can make it hard to get ready for bed and to fall asleep. You learned which part of the evening your worries show up most. You learned sleeping tips and how to watch bedtime worries. You practiced Laser Focus to grow calm and relaxed to fall asleep.

Go back and review your answers from the exercises in this chapter. Maybe ask a trusted adult about which ones they think helped you. Usually a sign that a superpower worked is if you were able to do something you had a hard time doing. Did you get ready for bed quickly without reminders? Did you stay in your bed after being tucked in? Let's make a plan to practice these for the next week so that you can strengthen these superpowers and keep your anxiety from getting in the way of falling asleep!

The next two exercises will also help with figuring out which exercises were helpful to you. Once you have a final list of superpowers, then you can plan to use them at bedtime this week. Keep up the good work!

MY FAVORITE BEDTIME SUPERPOWERS

SUPERPOWER: ....

Think about the different superpowers you learned in this chapter and the exercises you completed to practice them. You learned to face your worries by writing them down. You learned how to get unstuck from worries and how to sharpen your laser focus when getting ready for bed. A lot of the superpowers will require practice. So after you've practiced them, did you notice any change in how you feel? Maybe those situations aren't as uncomfortable anymore? Maybe you are getting ready for bed more easily, falling asleep more easily, or sleeping through the night? Those are all good signs that facing being uncomfortable has worked and has recalibrated your anxiety scanner so that it can continue being helpful. Pick the superpowers you found most helpful and draw them.

MY BEDTIME ACTION PLAN

SUPERPOWER: *BEING BRAVE*

It's time to make a bedtime action plan. With a plan, you will be prepared when worries show up at bedtime. Starting from the left, in the Situation column, write down what was happening when your worries showed up. In the My Worry column, write down what worries you at bedtime. In the My Exercise column, write down the name of one of your favorite exercises to deal with those worries. Finally, in the My Superpower column, write down which superpower that exercise belongs to. Let's complete one together.

SITUATION	MY WORRY	MY EXERCISE	MY SUPERPOWER
Brushing my teeth	What if I can't fall asleep tonight?	Bedtime Focus	Laser Focus

Now you fill in the rest!

SITUATION	MY WORRY	MY EXERCISE	MY SUPERPOWER

JUST FOR PARENTS

WHAT ARE CBT, ACT, AND MINDFULNESS?

This workbook uses skills from three therapeutic approaches: CBT, ACT, and Mindfulness. Let's review in more detail what each of these approaches mean and how they work to help your child.

Cognitive-Behavioral Therapy (CBT) is a change-oriented approach where your child learns to change some of their worries to more helpful thoughts. The CBT approach also helps your child face their anxiety. This would include doing things that your child may be avoiding. For example, learning to sleep without their night-light on if they are afraid of the dark. Learning to face anxiety is taught by taking small steps in facing their fears until they are ready to face the scariest fear last. For example, in the case of sleeping without a night-light, first your child might have the light off for one minute, and slowly work their way up to having it off all night. Facing fears should always be done with your child's agreement. Your child should not be "forced" into any of these activities. In this book CBT skills are the superpowers of Changing Worries and Being Brave.

Acceptance and Commitment Therapy (ACT) teaches your child how to relate differently to their worries. This approach is represented by the Getting Unstuck superpower. This is done by observing worries rather than trying to get rid of them. Your child also learns how to engage in activities that they care about despite experiencing worries. Often worries cause a child to stop doing things they like or cause your child to go above and beyond to ensure a certain outcome at the sacrifice of having fun. ACT helps your child reengage in doing fun things without worries getting in the way.

Mindfulness will help your child learn how to control their attention to stay focused on the present. In this book, mindfulness is referred to as the Laser Focus superpower. By being able to control their attention, your child is better able to shift their attention from anxiety-related thoughts to the present. For this reason, mindfulness is useful in a classroom setting. Your child can use it to focus on what the teacher is teaching instead of getting distracted by their worries. There are various exercises throughout the book that teach this skill.

TRACKING YOUR CHILD'S PROGRESS

Your child has tried a variety of skills to help manage their anxiety. Here is a chart that can help you track which exercises you feel helped your child. Generally, a good way to tell if a skill was helpful is if your child either changed their behavior or was able to manage their feeling of anxiety on their own.

EXERCISE	WAS THERE A CHANGE IN BEHAVIOR?	WAS YOUR CHILD ABLE TO HANDLE THEIR ANXIETY ON THEIR OWN?
Tweaking Your Anxiety Scanner	Yes	Yes

EXERCISE	WAS THERE A CHANGE IN BEHAVIOR?	WAS YOUR CHILD ABLE TO HANDLE THEIR ANXIETY ON THEIR OWN?

ARE YOU FEEDING YOUR CHILD'S ANXIETY?

An instinct that all parents have is to soothe and alleviate any pain or discomfort that their child experiences. It hurts to see your child in pain. So the most natural thing that you want to do is to help your child feel better. It's probably why you are reading this book. That approach, the need to make your child feel better, is the right one in almost all situations except in the case of anxiety. Sometimes parents with the best intentions can enable their children's anxiety. You may think, if my child asks a lot of reassurance-seeking questions, why not answer their questions if it makes them feel better? But the truth is that answering your child's reassurance-seeking questions can actually make their anxiety worse. By accommodating your child's anxious needs, you are feeding your child's anxiety and therefore making it worse in the long run. Before I explain how this works, I want to clarify that this approach is for anxious children who experience worries and anxiety consistently and whose anxiety interferes with their everyday functioning. This does not apply to children who experience anxiety infrequently and whose anxiety does not interfere with everyday functioning.

Providing reassurance to your child functions through a process called "negative reinforcement." It means that something unpleasant such as feeling anxious is removed (hence the term negative) by doing something (answering your child's questions). When you provide reassurance or accommodate anxious requests, your child becomes dependent on you to feel good. They learn that they cannot deal with their feelings on their own. As a parent, you want to teach your child how

to cope with their feelings; providing reassurance or being too accommodating can stunt this process.

If you allow your anxious child to stay home from school that day because they are avoiding giving a presentation, your anxious child learns that avoiding difficult situations is a healthy way of dealing with them. So, the next time there is something at school that causes anxiety for your child, your anxious child will want to stay home. This can set an unhealthy precedent for your anxious child.

What you probably already know is that once you start reassuring and accommodating, the requests don't stop; they keep coming. With time, answering a few questions doesn't work anymore, and they need to ask more and more questions to feel soothed and certain. This can cause a strain on your relationship with your child and likely their relationships with other people as well. In a nutshell, accommodating and providing reassurance is a short-term solution to dealing with your child's anxiety. What you need is a long-term solution. Try the next exercises to learn how.

IDENTIFYING YOUR CHILD'S ANXIOUS BEHAVIORS

Anxious behaviors are different for all kids. Some kids avoid while other kids ask reassuring questions. Here is a list of typical behaviors that parents often inadvertently reinforce. Circle which ones may be true for you and your child.

→ Answering questions about where you are going, who will be there, when you are leaving, and when you are returning home.

→ While you are away from your child, receiving calls/texts about when you will return.

→ Checking in on you at work.

→ Answering lots of "what-ifs."

→ Answering lots of "Are you sure that . . . (you will pick me up from school)?" or answering, "How do you know . . . (that my homework is fine)?" questions.

→ Allowing your child to stay home to avoid something at school like a presentation or a test.

→ Allowing your child to skip an after-school activity due to performance anxiety.

→ Needing to be in the same room as you.

→ Not being able to be in a room by themselves.

→ Asking you to check their homework over and over again.

→ Having to tuck them in or say goodnight a specific way. If the routine is out of order, your child gets anxious or requests to start it over again.

→ Other _

HELPING YOUR CHILD BREAK FREE FROM THEIR WORRY CYCLE

Let's review five ways you can break out of the reassurance/accommodating anxious cycle.

1. **LIMIT ANSWERING REASSURANCE-SEEKING QUESTIONS.** For example, if you are leaving to run an errand, provide your child with information about where you are going and when you will come back. After that, set a limit, such as three, for follow-up questions. Make sure it's a limit you can stick to. Consistency is important.

2. **DON'T LET YOUR CHILD AVOID.** If your child is anxious about something at school or at an after-school activity, they may want to avoid it. Be mindful of these situations and if you believe your child is avoiding an event because they are anxious, the best thing you can do is to encourage them to face it.

3. **USE A POINT OR STICKER REWARD SYSTEM FOR TASKS YOUR CHILD WANTS TO AVOID.** It's really hard to face things that make you anxious. Often children don't have the ability to look at the long-term benefits of facing their anxiety. Therefore, a reward system can help increase their motivation to face their anxiety.

4. **SHARE RESPONSIBILITIES WITH OTHERS IF POSSIBLE.** If your child asks for anxious accommodations from you but not from other adults, it may be best to pass that responsibility on to the other adult. For example, if at bedtime your child makes a lot of requests and avoids falling asleep when you tuck them in but not with someone else, have the other person be in charge of bedtime.

5. **SUGGEST SMALL CHANGES WHERE APPROPRIATE.** If your child has a specific bedtime routine that cannot be altered, see if your child would agree to changing the routine slightly. This can be as simple as changing the order of doing things or leaving one step out.

continued »»

Helping Your Child Break Free from Their Worry Cycle, *continued*

Circle the strategies you tried for at least a week and write down your impressions below:

INTERVENTION 1

Impact on my child's anxiety:

How difficult it was for you to implement:

INTERVENTION 2

Impact on my child's anxiety:

How difficult it was for you to implement:

Having a dedicated notebook or virtual document to track the efficacy of these interventions can help you to understand what works best over time.

Does Your Child Need More Support?

A good indicator that your child needs additional support from a professional is if your child's anxiety is interfering with their ability to do things they need to do (e.g., going to school and going to bed). If that is the case, you may want to find a professional who specializes in the approaches we discussed. Here are national organizations that have a list of such providers:

Anxiety and Depression Association of America (ADAA): ADAA.org

Association for Behavioral and Cognitive Therapies (ABCT): ABCT.org

Association for Contextual Behavioral Science (ACBS): ContextualScience.org/ACBS

MANAGING YOUR OWN ANXIETY

As a parent, you are the most influential person in your child's life. You are constantly teaching your child how to live in this world. This is one of the challenging and rewarding aspects of parenting. One thing to keep in mind as you are helping your child with their anxiety is to monitor your own emotions. This is important, because you are your child's main source of information about how to deal with feelings. There are two ways your own emotions can influence your child. One way is if you have your own anxiety about certain situations. As you know, children are like sponges and so they will pick up on your anxiety in those situations. Your child can learn from watching you be anxious about those situations, even if you think you are good at hiding it. You can tell this is happening if you start noticing similarities between your child's anxiety and your own.

The second way your emotions can influence your child's anxiety is your anticipatory anxiety about your child's anxiety. If you know that your child gets anxious before going to an after-school activity, you may start getting anxious around that time because you expect your child to be anxious as well. What ends up happening, though, is that your child then picks up on your anxiety, which sends your child the message that they are correct to be anxious about the after-school activity. Anxiety keeps getting exchanged back and forth in a feedback loop between you and your child. Your child picks up on your anxiety, so they think, "Oh, I guess there is something to worry about" and then you see your child's anxiety and think, "Oh no, he's getting anxious!" and back and forth it goes. Because you are the adult, it is up to you to break out of this anxious cycle.

In these scenarios, you may want to tap into some of your own skills to manage your own anxiety. If at all possible, take a skill that's in this book and show your child how you applied it to your own anxiety. This would be a great teaching moment and can help your child internalize the skills in this book. If you are having trouble managing your own anxiety, this may be an indication that you need additional support.

TRACKING YOUR ANXIETY ABOUT YOUR CHILD'S ANXIETY

Use the chart below to track your own anxiety about your child's anxiety. This chart will bring to your awareness situations that trigger your anxiety. Once you are aware of the situations and thoughts, it will give you a better idea of when to use skills to help you manage your own anxiety to help your child.

DAY	SITUATION	FEELING (1 TO 10; 1=LOW EMOTION, 10=HIGH EMOTION)	PHYSICAL SENSATIONS	THOUGHTS
Monday	Dropping my child off at their after-school activity	Anxious 7	Heart is pounding, sweating, and muscles are tense	Oh no! He's getting anxious. How do I stop this?

RESOURCES

BOOKS FOR KIDS

What to Do When You Worry Too Much: A Kid's Guide to Overcoming Anxiety by Dawn Huebner, PhD: This is a good book to read if you need more practice on how to deal with worries.

Nobody's Perfect: A Story for Children about Perfectionism by Ellen Flanagan Burns: This is a great book that can help if you worry too much about being perfect.

Up and Down the Worry Hill: A Children's Book about Obsessive-Compulsive Disorder and its Treatment by Aureen Pinto Wagner, PhD: This book can be helpful for kids that get stuck doing and thinking things over and over again.

BOOKS FOR PARENTS

Anxious Kids, Anxious Parents: 7 Ways to Stop the Worry Cycle and Raise Courageous and Independent Children by Reid Wilson, PhD and Lynn Lyons, LICSW

Helping Your Anxious Child: A Step-by-Step Guide for Parents by Ronald M. Rapee, PhD, Ann Wignall, D.Psych, Susan H. Spence, PhD, Vanessa Cobham, PhD, and Heidi Lyneham, PhD

CopingCatparents.com/Child_Anxiety_Tales

Parenting program developed by Dr. Philip Kendal and Dr. Muniya Khanna. This is an online parent training program for parents of anxious children.

You and Your Anxious Child: Free Your Child from Fears and Worries and Create a Joyful Family Life by Anne Marie Albano, PhD, and Leslie Pepper

INDEX

ACKNOWLEDGMENTS

I would like to thank my family and friends for their love and support. To my parents for making sure I am fed and to my friends for ensuring I take breaks from writing. I am grateful to my past and present clients who work so hard to accept and change their feelings and behaviors. They teach and inspire me every week.

ABOUT THE AUTHOR

DR. AGNES SELINGER, PhD, is a clinical psychologist with a dual doctorate degree in school and clinical psychology. She specializes in the treatment of anxiety and depression across the life span using third-wave therapies such as CBT, ACT, and Mindfulness-Based CBT. Dr. Selinger is in private practice in Manhattan. Read more about Dr. Selinger at AgnesSelingerPhD.com.

Anxiety Relief Workbook for Kids